Jesus shed His **BLOOD** to s

We do good deeds to honor God. Find and circle the words on the list.

GOOD DEEDS WORD FIND

```
P K C I S E H T T I S I V S
J R P G G C G J L W G W T M
E X A P O M L T P I D N M J
T L P Y L T Z E V P E T Z B
D P B P F J O E A R J Y T R
D J B A N O T C A N R Q D L
R G Z Z T O R P H B R R L B
G M V J P T R F T U M O Y B
Z D N O L O E Q R R R J O Y
G N O Z N R S Q I R C Y M
P R M O J B R L L E M H L
X T H J V Y Q K Y G B N J D
J W G M P W L K M N V Q D Z
```

HONOR PARENTS
GO TO CHURCH
VISIT THE SICK
CLEAN ROOM
PRAY FOR FRIEND
GIVE TO POOR
SET TABLE

TALK ABOUT IT...

What is a good deed that you can do today?

Jesus carried His cross to the hill of CALVARY.

Connect the dots around the cross. Color the cloth purple and cross brown. Purple represents the Lenten season. On Easter morning the cloth is changed to white.

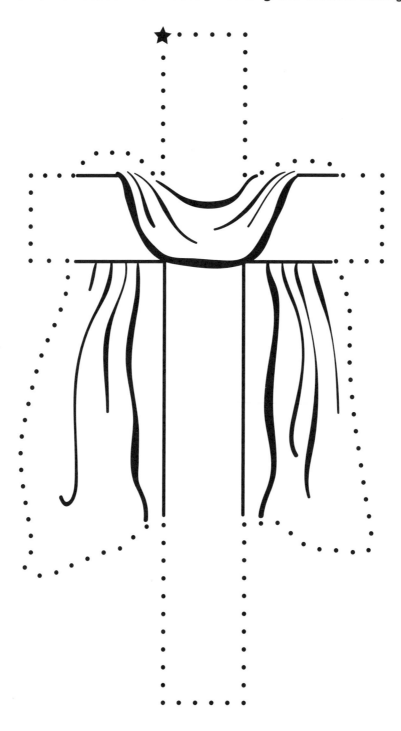

Jesus arrived in Jerusalem riding a DONKEY.

Learn to draw a donkey! Using a sheet of copy paper, follow the directions to create your donkey. Tracing over the book copy will help get you started. When you are finished, draw the scene where Jesus arrives in the city of Jerusalem.

Draw an oval shape for the body and head.
Connect with lines to make the neck.

Add ears. Add a circle with dot for the eye.
Add muzzle line, dot for nose and smile.
Add legs and hoof lines.

Add a tail and mane.

Erase the lines to match the donkey above.
Congratulations!
Your donkey is ready to color!

E

On EASTER we celebrate the EMPTY tomb!

*Jesus is known by many wonderful names!
Find and circle the names from the list at the bottom.*

JESUS IS...

```
N E S O H C D C D O G F O B M A L P B B
A N V D W N Y R O X J G P A N W L L Q K
G G P T M O M R T U D R L Z O Z R J J M
N D E W N I Y G B N M O N P N J M Y R
R A V M Y T B L R B I S D I E X Z D E Y
E E G J O A E X Y G E E E N V Z G T L J
M R L M Z D Z M H T R L O L V A N B R M
E B L Y R N N T M F S T O Z O E S E Y P
E X H T B U Y A U A S I T V P R V B X A
D L H O J O A L A R N D R R E E D K P M
E D G C L F W D E H O U A H R D I O E K
R G E N N Y D N V G P C E L C N S S C Q
R E P L P A R Y F O M L A L G T S O Y J
Z D T Z I O R O L T C S A O L I R Z N V
J J T S C V N B Q M T A F E A Q Q X J V
R E R Y A O E G K I Q K T H X D B M B W
W M S T S M Y R N D I D V E N Y M M B Q
Q X N U Z Z J G E N P Y Z Q M D A Q M D
J Y Z L S Q D Q G R L Y Q Z T I Z Q M R
R D G J N L M S M Y T R M N M X D T J X
```

ADVOCATE	**CORNERSTONE**	**KING OF KINGS**
ALMIGHTY	**COUNSELOR**	**LAMB OF GOD**
ALPHA AND OMEGA	**DELIVERER**	**MESSIAH**
BELOVED SON	**EMMANUEL**	**MASTER**
BRANCH	**EVERLASTING**	**REDEEMER**

TALK ABOUT IT...

What is your favorite name for Jesus?

 Jesus FORGIVES our sin. We are to FOLLOW His example and FORGIVE others, too.

Write different ways to forgive others in each heart. Color the picture.

TALK ABOUT IT...

What does it mean to forgive others?

GOOD Friday is the Friday before Easter. It is called "GOOD Friday" because Jesus demonstrated His great love for us by dying for our sins.

Color the picture bright colors.

TALK ABOUT IT...

How will you share the good news about Jesus with others?

When Jesus arrived in Jerusalem, the people shouted "HOSANNA in the highest!" They placed palm fronds on the street.

Connect the dots around the palm frond. Color and carefully cut out.

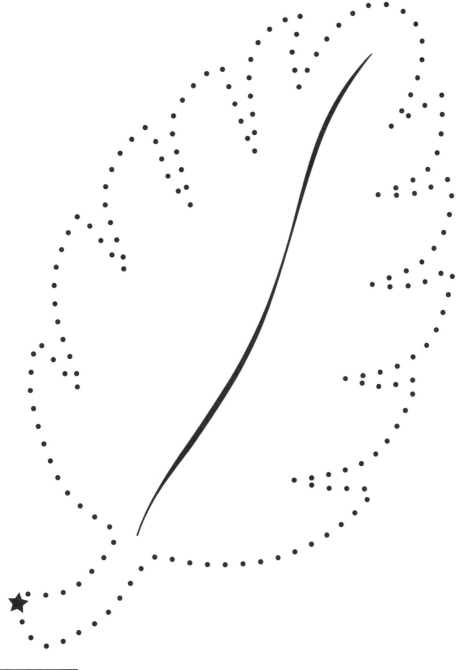

TALK ABOUT IT...

Wave the palm frond and shout "Hosanna in the highest!"

 It pleases Jesus when we live a life that **IMITATES** His.

What can you do to follow Jesus this week? Perhaps you can start with "be kind to others". Write down your answers and color in the footprint each day.

JUDAS, one of the apostles, betrayed Jesus.

Judas was lost, but Jesus is the star of our hearts! Find your way through the maze. Color the picture in bright colors.

Jesus was mocked and called KING of the Jews.

*Jesus is the Prince of Peace! Find the following hidden items and color the picture:
bird, bell, beanie, umbrella, fish, cup, moon*

 **LENT** is the period of forty days prior to Easter Sunday. It is a time of fasting from certain foods or activities, praying and repentance. It reminds us of the forty days that Jesus fasted in the wilderness.

Color the picture. In the rays around Jesus, add words that describe God.

M MOTHER MARY'S heart was broken.

Fill in the blanks with the beginning letter of each object.

TALK ABOUT IT...
Share this message with everyone you meet!

On the cross, NAILS were driven into Jesus' hands and feet.

Find and circle the words from the list below.

```
N S M G G N L D M G T L R Z D J D
O L T L R G G D J K E E T Z V Z R
I E S L I A N R D K C X Z J T N Y
T G V R L X Y T A I Y E L P M E T
C N Y G T G X U F R B D J J N M R
E A X J R B Q I A V N T J K G P Q
R Y K J J H R V N D B E E Y I R K
R N B Q T C L M N G S T Y L O N Z
U D Z R A A V K M U A K B M I L G
S M A S C Z B V S L M K A M Z F M
E E C R O S S C I B E N D M A Z E
R S P E A R H P M K S V O E M L J
T R N Y D R Y O A T D T O G A M K
D X Y R I K T Y R N N P L L Z T X
W X M S K W L Z Y G G Q B Q Z V H
N Z T T D Z N N L L B X D Q K V Y
```

CROSS	KING	DEATH	SACRIFICE
NAILS	PILATE	LIFE	TEMPLE
EARTHQUAKE	CALVARY	LOVE	SPEAR
JESUS CHRIST	BLOOD	ROMANS	TOMB
LAMB	ANGELS	RESURRECTION	MARY

TALK ABOUT IT...

What does the Resurrection mean to you?

The **OPEN** tomb is what Easter is all about.

Color the starred areas red and the rest of the spaces in bright colors.

TALK ABOUT IT...

Hang it up as a reminder of how much Jesus loves you!

PENTECOST is when the disciples received God's Holy Spirit, as Jesus had promised.

The Holy Spirit hears us when we pray. Connect the dots around the hands and color the picture.

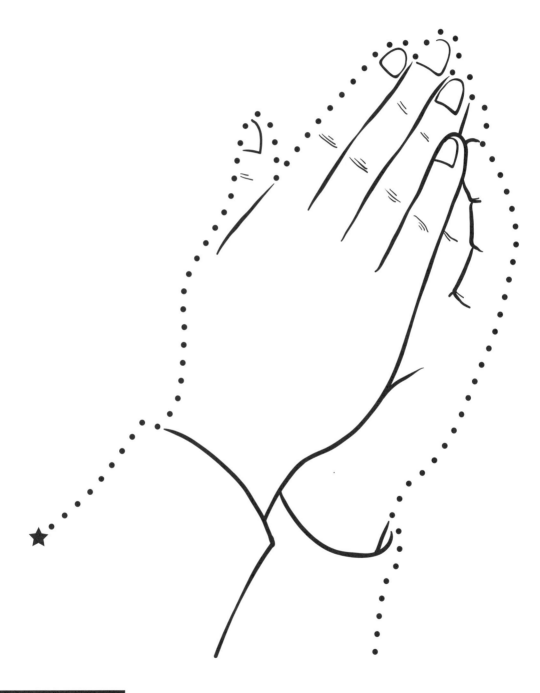

TALK ABOUT IT...
What will you pray for today?

 Mary Magdalene meets Jesus at the tomb and QUICKLY goes to tell the disciples what He said.

Greeting people at church is fun! How many silly things can you find? Color the picture.

 The **RESURRECTION** of Jesus means that we have new life through sacrifice.

God is love! How many hearts can you find? Color the picture.

 The Last SUPPER is the meal that Jesus shared with His disciples to celebrate the Passover.

Talk about the Last Supper and Passover. Decorate the chalice and color the picture. In the blank area, write your prayer for today.

Jesus **TEACHES** His disciples that God loved us so much that He sent His one and only Son, Jesus, into the world, to die for all people, to save us from our sins.

Jesus promises us that He will never leave us. Find and circle the words from the list. Color the picture.

**JESUS   PETER   COURAGE   PRAY   WIND   WAVES   DOUBT
SINK   WATER   ALONE   WALKING   FAITH   STORM   AFRAID**

TALK ABOUT IT...

Do you know the Bible story of this puzzle?

U Jesus ascended UP into heaven to be with God.

Look at the objects on the cross. In the blank spaces, write the first letter of the object. The first 2 are done for you. Color the picture.

I

T _ _ _ _ _

_ _ _ _ .

The **VEIL** in the temple was torn in two the moment Jesus died.

We are thankful we have a personal relationship with Jesus! What are you thankful for today? Think about it as you color the picture.

Jesus **WASHED** His disciple's feet. He explained that He came to serve others. To be like Jesus, we are called to love and serve others.

Count your blessings! Write or draw your blessings in the space to the left. Draw one of the many ways you can bless others on the right.

 We are EXTRA happy because Jesus is our friend!

Jesus loves me! Color the picture.

TALK ABOUT IT...

Hang it where you can share the message with others.

 He died for YOU and me, to forgive us of our sins.

Look at the picture on the top. Circle all of the differences in the picture on the bottom. Color the picture.

TALK ABOUT IT...

What does it mean to be a good friend?

Lightning bolts ZAPPED across a darkened sky while Jesus hung on the cross.

Color the picture.

TALK ABOUT IT...

How many hidden lightning bolts can you find?

COLOR EACH JELLYBEAN TO MATCH THE COLOR WORD NEXT TO IT.

The Jellybean Prayer

○ Red is for the blood Jesus gave on the cross.

○ Green is for the palms waved as He entered Jerusalem.

○ Yellow is for God's light that shines in our heart.

○ Orange is for the prayers we say at bedtime.

○ Black is for the rest that He provides.

○ White is for the grace of Christ which He freely gives.

○ Purple is for His days of sorrow.

○ Pink is for the joy of each new day.

AMEN!

JESUS IS THE LIGHT OF MY HEART.

Color the picture.

ADD A CROSS ON THE STEEPLE.

Add doors. Add stained glass windows. Add your and your family, too. Color the picture.

TALK ABOUT IT...

What did you learn this week at Mass?

LOOK AT THE PICTURE ON THE TOP.

*Circle all of the differences in the picture on the bottom.
Color the picture.*

TALK ABOUT IT...
Spend time today reading God's Word!

WE SHOULD THINK OF JESUS OFTEN AND THANK HIM FOR ALL HE HAS DONE FOR US.

Learn to sign "Thank You, Jesus." Practice the motions and share with someone.

THANK YOU

The sign for "thank you" is made by putting the fingers of your dominant hand near your lips. Your hand should be a "flat" hand. Next, move your hand forward, down a bit, in the direction of the person you are speaking with. Remember to smile!

It's like blowing a kiss without puckering your lips!

JESUS

The sign for "Jesus" is done by touching the tip of the middle finger on your dominant hand into the center of your palm of your other hand. Then touch the tip of your middle finger of your non-dominant hand into the palm of your dominant hand.

Think of the nails through Jesus' palms while He was on the cross.

TALK ABOUT IT...

Can learning sign language help you tell hearing impaired people about God?

An **ANGEL** appeared at the empty tomb and said, "Do not be afraid! Jesus is not here. He is risen, just as He said!"

Write the words the angel said in the text bubble. Color the picture.

TALK ABOUT IT...

In your own words, describe what that moment might have been like.

Easter A-Z

Easter is the celebration of Christ's resurrection from the dead. He is risen! It's the best news ever! God loved us so much that He sent His Son, Jesus, to die for all people and save us from our sin. Praise God for His amazing gift!

Let's learn a little more about the story of Easter.
It's as easy as ABC!

Written and Illustrated by Deborah C. Johnson
ISBN 978-1-61796-211-0
© 2017 Aquinas Kids, Phoenix, Arizona
Printed in China